A Midsummr Night's Disaster

Written by Adam and Charlotte Guillain

RISING★STARS

Chapter 1: News of the Play

"I bumped into my friend Janice today," Asha's dad told Asha and her friends. "Her theatre company is looking for some children to be in their play."

Asha and Tess exchanged an excited look.

"The play is *A Midsummer Night's Dream* and they need fairies," Asha's dad explained.

"Can we be in it?" chorused the friends.

"As it's the summer holidays, I don't see why not," said Asha's dad, "but let's go inside and ask your parents."

Everyone agreed it was an excellent idea, so Asha's dad rang Janice.

"You can join the rehearsal tomorrow," he told the friends.

Yes!

"What's *A Midsummer Night's Dream* about?" asked Finn.

"We've got a picture book that tells you the story," said Rav's mum, and she went to fetch it. The friends sat on the sofa and looked at the book.

"It's in a forest with fairies and magic," said Asha, her eyes sparkling.

The next day, Asha's dad took the four friends to the theatre.

"Hello!" said a smiley woman. "I'm Janice, the director of the play. Thank you for coming!"

The friends introduced themselves.

"You'll make perfect fairies," said Janice. "Let's find you some costumes."

The costumes were so leafy they almost looked like plants! Asha, Rav, Tess and Finn concentrated hard as they did what Janice asked them to do.

"Tomorrow is the final rehearsal before the play opens for a week," Janice told them when Asha's dad came to pick them up.

I can't wait!

Chapter 2: Clang!

The next day, the rehearsal started off well.

"Fairies, you need to come on with the fairy queen," called Janice, and the friends ran onto the stage.

"Don't hide behind that tree, Finn!" whispered Tess.

"Try not to be nervous," hissed Rav, and Finn shuffled out to stand next to his friends.

Suddenly, there was an enormous CLANG!

Everyone jumped. "What was that?" gasped Finn.

Janice waved from the seat where she was watching the rehearsal. "Ignore it," she called. "Just go on."

Tess was getting ready to say her line when … CLANG!

"What is going on?" groaned Janice, jumping up to find out what the noise was. A man poked his head round from the back of the theatre.

"Sorry about the noise!" he shouted. "There's a problem with the water pipes. I'm just trying to get everything fixed before tomorrow's performance."

"Do you think you could do it quietly?" asked Janice. "We need to rehearse in here."

"I'll try my best," said the man, waving his spanner as he left the room.

Janice put her hand to her head and frowned.

"What's wrong?" asked one of the actors.

Janice sighed. "We won't be able to open up to the public tomorrow if the water pipes aren't working," she said, "and the theatre really needs to make money from this play – it will be a disaster if we can't perform."

Janice clapped her hands. "Let's get on with the rehearsal," she said.

The actors got back into position on the stage and the fairy queen smiled at Tess.

"My turn to speak!" Tess thought, and opened her mouth to say her line, but before she could speak there was an enormous bang!

Bang!

Chapter 3: A Disaster

Everyone froze. Janice stood up and looked at the back of the theatre but nobody appeared.

"It sounds like they've finished," she called. "Let's carry on."

They continued with the rehearsal and watched the fairy king step on to the stage.

Finn twitched as he felt something cold run down his neck. He looked across at Rav, who was wiping his eye and frowning.

"Is something dripping on the stage?" asked the fairy king.

Tess looked up and a drop of water splashed on her face.

"Oh no," murmured Asha.

Janice ran up the steps on to the stage and stared at a puddle growing on the floor.

"What's happening?" she shouted.

Water was dripping down on them faster now.

"My costume's getting ruined!" cried the fairy queen.

A face appeared at the back of the theatre. It was the man with the spanner.

"Um, we seem to have a bigger problem than we realised," said the man as he walked on to the stage.

"What does that mean?" bellowed Janice.

"Well, it's the pipes, you see," the man started to say.

SPLASH!

A torrent of water plummeted down on to the stage.

"Help!" shrieked Janice.

Chapter 4: Asha's Idea

Everyone leaped off the stage and ran towards the back of the theatre. Water was dripping from the ceiling and running down the walls.

"This is a disaster," groaned Janice. "We can't use the theatre like this, and the play starts tomorrow!"

Could the play wait until the pipes are fixed?

"It'll take us at least a week to fix this," said the man with the spanner.

"We can't wait a week," Janice wailed. "We've sold all the tickets and we need the money to keep the theatre running."

One of the actors put his arm on her shoulder.

Everyone stared at the floor in silence. "Do you think the play's going to happen?" Asha whispered to Tess. Tess shrugged.

Janice looked up with disappointed eyes. "We're going to have to pack up," she said. "We'll have to cancel the play and give everyone who bought tickets their money back."

Janice called Asha's dad to collect them. "What a shame!" he said when he heard the news.

"I was really looking forward to our first performance," sighed Finn as they trudged home.

As they walked through the woods near the theatre, Asha grabbed Rav's arm.

I think I've got an idea!

Chapter 5: A Midsummer Night's Dream

"What is it?" asked Tess.

"The play is set in a wood, isn't it?" said Asha. The others nodded. "So why don't we perform the play here?" she went on.

Rav's face lit up. "What a great idea!" he said.

"What would the audience sit on?" asked Asha's dad.

Finn looked around. "There are plenty of logs for people to use as benches," he said.

"Some people could bring deckchairs too," suggested Tess.

"That space over there could be the stage," said Asha.

Her dad smiled. "I think it might just work!" he said.

When they got home, Asha's dad rang Janice.

"She thinks it's a brilliant idea," said Asha's dad as he put his phone down. Asha ran to hug him.

An hour later, there was a knock at Asha's flat.

Janice came in, beaming. "It's going to be magical!" she cried.

"Now, there's lots to do!" Janice told Asha's dad. They spent the rest of the afternoon making phone calls to get permission to use the woods and contacting all the actors and the crew.

"See you tomorrow, bright and early!" called Janice as she waved goodbye.

The next day, they went to the woods straight after breakfast.

"Let's put the logs out in rows," said Finn.

Soon, people were arranging pieces of scenery and hanging lights in the trees.

"My mum's at the theatre calling everyone with tickets," Rav told his friends. "She's telling them to come here instead."

They worked hard all day, getting the woods ready and having a final rehearsal.

"I hope it goes well," said Janice. "I've never directed a play in a wood before."

Soon, the audience was streaming through the trees. The friends went and said hello to their parents before they went backstage.

Before they knew it, the play had started.

"Let's go!" whispered Tess as the fairy king and queen swept past.

Finn's hands were shaking as they ran onstage but a happy warmth spread over him as he said his line and the audience laughed and clapped.

At the end, everyone stood up to clap and cheer the actors.

"That was brilliant!" said Rav as they left the stage, glowing with happiness.

"My fairies really can perform magic!" said Janice. "You were amazing. Now, where's Asha?"

Asha stepped forwards and Janice handed her a headband made of flowers and leaves.

Wow, thank you!

"No! Thank *you*!" said Janice. "Your brilliant idea saved our play."

"You can use that for your school project," suggested Tess. Their class had to collect six things to remember the summer holidays by.

"I can't wait to do it all again tomorrow," said Finn with a grin.

A Midsummer Night's Disaster

What other things will the Comet Street Kids collect for their holiday challenge? Read the other books in this band to find out!

A Midsummer Night's Disaster

The Missing Cat

Moonquake

Brilliant Braille

Stop Shouting!

Stranded Panda

Talk about the story

Answer the questions:

1 Who did Asha's dad 'bump into' at the start of the story?

2 What characters were the friends going to be in the play?

3 What does the word 'director' mean? (page 5)

4 Why was there an 'enormous CLANG' on page 8?

5 Where did Asha suggest they should perform the play?

6 Why was the performance of the play in the woods at the end?

7 How do you think Janice felt when she thought they'd have to cancel the play?

8 Have you ever performed in a play? What part did you play?

Can you retell the story in your own words?